footprints

SCRIPTURE *with* REFLECTIONS

for Men

INSPIRED *by the* BEST-LOVED POEM

EVERY NOW AND THEN DURING our devotional time my husband, Paul, and I reread the poem I wrote for him back in 1964. During these times of renewal and prayer, we talk over the events of our lives and share burdens we have for ourselves and others. Very often, we realize that the Great Shepherd has once again reached out and carried us through the day as we spend these introspective moments together.

If the pleasure of sharing these thoughts anew has taught us anything, it is this: that God's Word is true. Our Heavenly Father is faithful and will never leave us or forsake us. As we come to Him daily, willing to be shaped and directed, His Word gives guideposts of clear direction. Almost everything we read, see, and experience shows us in some way that, although we do not visibly see God, He is with us. Over centuries of time others have looked back to understand that God's Spirit and presence were there, even when they felt alone.

In our quiet moments of reflection, in the fellowship of others and even in dreams, God opens the doors to our hearts. This is what happened when I originally wrote the poem, "Footprints."

After hours of wrestling with the darkness of doubt and despair, I finally surrendered to Him and, in the early morning light of peace, wrote the poem as result of that spiritual experience.

Listen for the gentle stirring of God's grace in your own mind and soul as you read these verses of encouragement. Each of us is different in our spiritual need, just as each of our days is different. God wants to place His signature on your life in a unique way. As you spend time, even just a few moments each day, reflecting on His Word, it will help you to know Him better.

Spiritual growth is not so much what we have done, but the feeling of love for Him we put into everything we do. It is not so much in knowing about God that we grow, but in getting to know Him in a personal, relational way. It is in becoming "a friend of God," as Abraham did, that we grow in His grace, talking with Him as our companion along the way, letting God sift our thoughts and plans through the standards of His Word. May these verses encourage you anew each day as you walk with Him.

Margaret Fishback Powers

footprints

One night I dreamed a dream.
I was walking along the beach with my Lord.
Across the dark sky flashed scenes from my life.
For each scene, I noticed two sets of footprints in the sand,
one belonging to me and one to my Lord.
When the last scene of my life shot before me
I looked back at the footprints in the sand
and to my surprise,
I noticed that many times along the path of my life
there was only one set of footprints.
I realized that this was at the lowest
and saddest times of my life.
This always bothered me
and I questioned the Lord about my dilemma.
"Lord, you told me when I decided to follow You,
You would walk and talk with me all the way.
But I'm aware that during the most troublesome
times of my life there is only one set of footprints.
I just don't understand why, when I needed You most,
You leave me."
He whispered, "My precious child,
I love you and will never leave you
never, ever, during your trials and testings.
When you saw only one set of footprints
it was then that I carried you."

© 1964 MARGARET FISHBACK POWERS

GOD IS *with* US...

PROVIDING INSIGHT *and* UNDERSTANDING

One night I dreamed a dream.

S ome of our dreams can have a powerful effect on us. All of us have, at one time or another, awakened laughing or fretful—and all because of a dream. The Bible tells us about many people who had dreams and visions that were given to them by God …

The LORD appeared to Solomon during the night in a dream. … God gave Solomon wisdom and very great insight, and a breadth of understanding as measureless as the sand on the seashore.

1 KINGS 3:5; 4:29

[Jacob] had a dream in which he saw a stairway resting on the earth, with its top reaching to heaven, and the angels of God were ascending and descending on it. There above it stood the LORD, and he said: "I am the LORD, the God of your father Abraham and the God of Isaac. … I am with you and will watch over you wherever you go."

GENESIS 28:12−13, 15

An angel of the Lord appeared to [Joseph] in a dream and said, "Joseph son of David, do not be afraid to take Mary home as your wife, because what is conceived in her is from the Holy Spirit. She will give birth to a son, and you are to give him the name Jesus, because he will save his people from their sins."

MATTHEW 1:20−21

In the year that King Uzziah died, I saw the Lord, seated on a throne, high and exalted, and the train of his robe filled the temple.

ISAIAH 6:1

One day at about three in the afternoon [Cornelius] had a vision. He distinctly saw an angel of God. …[He later told Peter,] "Suddenly a man in shining clothes stood before me and said, 'Cornelius, God has heard your prayer and remembered your gifts to the poor. Send to Joppa for Simon who is called Peter.' … So I sent for you immediately, and it was good of you to come. Now we are all here in the presence of God to listen to everything the Lord has commanded you to tell us."

ACTS 10:3, 30–33

On the Lord's Day I was in the Spirit, and I heard behind me a loud voice like a trumpet. …And when I turned I saw … someone "like a son of man," dressed in a robe reaching down to his feet and with a golden sash around his chest. His head and hair were white like wool, as white as snow, and his eyes were like blazing fire. … He placed his right hand on me and said: "Do not be afraid. I am the First and the Last. I am the Living One; I was dead, and behold I am alive for ever and ever! And I hold the keys of death and Hades."

REVELATION 1:10, 12–14, 17–18

Samuel went and lay down in his place.
The LORD came and stood there, calling, …
"Samuel! Samuel!"
Then Samuel said, "Speak, for your servant is
listening."
And the Lord said to Samuel: "See, I am about to
do something in Israel that will make the ears of
everyone who hears of it tingle."

I SAMUEL 3:9–11

The word of the LORD came to Abram in a vision:
"Do not be afraid, Abram.
  I am your shield,
    your very great reward."

GENESIS 15:1

While I was still in prayer, Gabriel, the man I had seen
in the earlier vision, came to me in swift flight. … He
instructed me and said to me, "Daniel, I have now come
to give you insight and understanding. As soon as you
began to pray, an answer was given, which I have come
to tell you, for you are highly esteemed."

DANIEL 9:21–23

We should not ignore our dreams. God will
sometimes use our dreams to assure us of his
promises or to tell us something about himself.
And when God does speak to us in dreams, he
will also help us understand them.

God said, "Listen to my words:
"When a prophet of the LORD is among you,
   I reveal myself to him in visions,
   I speak to him in dreams."

NUMBERS 12:6

"I will pour out my Spirit on all people.
Your sons and daughters will prophesy,
   your old men will dream dreams,
   your young men will see visions,"
      declares the Lord.

JOEL 2:28

[Joseph] asked Pharaoh's officials who were in custody with him in his master's house, "Why are your faces so sad today?"
"We both had dreams," they answered, "but there is no one to interpret them."
Then Joseph said to them, "Do not interpretations belong to God? Tell me your dreams."

GENESIS 40:7–8

There is a God in heaven who reveals mysteries.

DANIEL 2:28

Pharaoh said to Joseph, "I had a dream, and no one can interpret it. But I have heard it said of you that when you hear a dream you can interpret it."
"I cannot do it," Joseph replied to Pharaoh, "but God will give Pharaoh the answer he desires."

GENESIS 41:15–16

The Lord will give you insight.

2 TIMOTHY 2:7

God's presence with us is a reality. It is a dream come true.... As we dream our dreams with the knowledge that God is with us, we will begin to see things as Christ does and dream dreams inspired by the Holy Spirit that are worth retelling and following.

"I know the plans I have for you," declares the LORD, *"plans to prosper you and not to harm you, plans to give you hope and a future."*

JEREMIAH 29:11

Joseph had a dream. ... He said to [his brothers], "Listen to this dream I had: We were binding sheaves of grain out in the field when suddenly my sheaf rose and stood upright, while your sheaves gathered around mine and bowed down to it. ..." Then he had another dream, and he told it to his brothers. "Listen," he said, "I had another dream, and this time the sun and moon and eleven stars were bowing down to me."

GENESIS 37:5-7, 9

[Paul said,] "As I was on the road, I saw a light from heaven, brighter than the sun, blazing around me and my companions. We all fell to the ground, and I heard a voice saying to me in Aramaic ... 'I am Jesus, whom you are persecuting. ... I have appeared to you to appoint you as a servant and as a witness.'"

ACTS 26:13-16

When life caves in, you do not need reasons, you need comfort. You do not need some answers; you need someone. And Jesus does not come to us with an explanation; he comes to us with his presence.

We are always seeking the reason. We want to know why. Like Job, we finally want God to tell us just what is going on. …

But God does not reveal his plan, he reveals himself. He comes to us as warmth when we are cold, fellowship when we are alone, strength when we are weak, peace when we are troubled, and courage when we are afraid.

He is with us on our journeys. He is there when we are home. He sits with us at our table. He knows about funerals and weddings and commencements and hospitals and jails and unemployment and labor and laughter and rest and tears. He knows because he is with us. He comes to us again and again.

BOB BENSON

GOD *is* WITH US...

in OUR DAILY WALK

*I was walking along the beach
with my Lord.*

A CLOSE WALK WITH THE LORD is an important part of a believer's life.

May God turn our hearts to him, to walk in all his ways and to keep the commands, decrees and regulations he gave our fathers.

1 KINGS 8:58

Your love is ever before me, Lord,
*   and I walk continually in your truth.*

PSALM 26:3

Walk in the way of understanding.

PROVERBS 9:6

He whose walk is upright fears the LORD.

PROVERBS 14:2

The ways of the LORD are right;
*   the righteous walk in them.*

HOSEA 14:9

He whose walk is blameless is kept safe.

PROVERBS 28:18

Let us walk in the light of the LORD.

ISAIAH 2:5

The Bible tells us that maintaining a close walk with God is a command we must obey, not merely a suggestion we may want to consider.

"I am God Almighty; walk before me and be blameless."

What does the Lord your God ask of you but to fear the Lord your God, to walk in all his ways, to love him, to serve the Lord your God with all your heart and with all your soul?

Deuteronomy 10:12

Love the Lord your God ... walk in all his ways ... hold fast to him.

Deuteronomy 11:22

The Lord will establish you ... if you keep the commands of the Lord your God and walk in his ways.

Deuteronomy 28:9

You saw how the Lord your God carried you, as a father carries his son.

Deuteronomy 1:31

God has showed you, O man, what is good.
    And what does the Lord require of you?
To act justly and to love mercy
    and to walk humbly with your God.

MICAH 6:8

This is love: that we walk in obedience to God's com-
mands. As you have heard from the beginning, his
command is that you walk in love.

2 JOHN 6

"Obey me, and I will be your God and you will be
my people. Walk in all the ways I command you, that
it may go well with you."

JEREMIAH 7:23

Be very careful to keep the commandment and the law
that Moses the servant of the LORD gave you: to love
the LORD your God, to walk in all his ways, to obey
his commands, to hold fast to him and to serve him
with all your heart and all your soul.

JOSHUA 22:5

But what does a walk with God actually entail?
How does God want us to live?

Love the LORD *your God with all your heart and*
with all your soul and with all your strength. These
commandments that I give you today are to be upon
your hearts. Impress them on your children. Talk about
them when you sit at home and when you walk along
the road, when you lie down and when you get up.

DEUTERONOMY 6:5–7

LORD, *who may dwell in your sanctuary?*
   Who may live on your holy hill?
He whose walk is blameless
   and who does what is righteous,
who speaks the truth from his heart
   and has no slander on his tongue,
who does his neighbor no wrong
   and casts no slur on his fellowman,
who despises a vile man
   but honors those who fear the LORD,
who keeps his oath
   even when it hurts,
who lends his money without usury
   and does not accept a bribe against the innocent.
He who does these things
   will never be shaken.

PSALM 15

Many of these things that God asks us to do go against our nature. The Bible urges us to consistently walk with the Lord, walking by faith, even when it's difficult.

Live a life worthy of the Lord ... please him in every way: bearing fruit in every good work, growing in the knowledge of God, ... and joyfully giving thanks to the Father, who has qualified you to share in the inheritance of the saints in the kingdom of light.

COLOSSIANS 1:10–12

Just as you received Christ Jesus as Lord, continue to live in him, rooted and built up in him, strengthened in the faith as you were taught, and overflowing with thankfulness.

COLOSSIANS 2:6–7

If we walk in the light, as God is in the light, we have fellowship with one another, and the blood of Jesus, his Son, purifies us from all sin.

1 JOHN 1:7

I pray that out of God's glorious riches he may strengthen you with power through his Spirit in your inner being.

EPHESIANS 3:16

Jesus said, *"Walk while you have the light, before darkness overtakes you. The man who walks in the dark does not know where he is going. Put your trust in the light while you have it, so that you may become sons of light."*

JOHN 12:35–36

Live a life of love, just as Christ loved us and gave himself up for us.

EPHESIANS 5:2

Health professionals suggest that people who want to become physically fit should try a consistent program of walking. Sustained walking several times a week will improve your muscle tone and strengthen your heart.

The Bible reassures us that our spiritual lives will also reap benefits when we are consistent in walking with the Lord. Look at the many benefits a walk with God provides.

Walk in all the way that the LORD your God has commanded you, so that you may live and prosper and prolong your days in the land that you will possess.

DEUTERONOMY 5:33

I command you today to love the LORD your God, to walk in his ways, and to keep his commands, decrees and laws; then you will live and increase, and the LORD your God will bless you.

DEUTERONOMY 30:16

Observe what the LORD your God requires: Walk in his ways ... so that you may prosper in all you do and wherever you go.

1 KINGS 2:3

The LORD God is a sun and shield;
*   the LORD bestows favor and honor;*
no good thing does he withhold
*   from those whose walk is blameless.*

PSALM 84:11

"If you walk in my ways and obey my statutes and commands ... I will give you a long life," says the Lord.

1 KINGS 3:14

From everlasting to everlasting
*   the LORD's love is with those who fear him,*
*   and his righteousness with their*
*   children's children—*
with those who keep his covenant
*   and remember to obey his precepts.*

PSALM 103:17–18

Blessed are all who fear the LORD,
   who walk in his ways.
You will eat the fruit of your labor;
   blessings and prosperity will be yours.

PSALM 128:1–2

God holds victory in store for the upright,
   he is a shield to those whose walk is blameless.

PROVERBS 2:7

Blessed is the man
   who does not walk in the counsel of the wicked
or stand in the way of sinners
   or sit in the seat of mockers.
But his delight is in the law of the LORD,
   and on his law he meditates day and night.
He is like a tree planted by streams of water,
   which yields its fruit in season
and whose leaf does not wither.
   Whatever he does prospers.

PSALM 1:1–3

This is what the LORD says:
"Stand at the crossroads and look;
   ask for the ancient paths,
ask where the good way is, and walk in it,
   and you will find rest for your souls."

JEREMIAH 6:16

Blessed are they whose ways are blameless,
    who walk according to the law of the LORD.
Blessed are they who keep his statutes
    and seek him with all their heart.
They do nothing wrong;
    they walk in his ways.

PSALM 119:1–3

The Bible begins to give us some clues about godliness in its earliest pages. Genesis 5:21–24 tells us about Enoch, the father of Methuselah. In a very short three-verse summary of Enoch's life, Moses twice describes him as one who "walked with God." The author of Hebrews gives Enoch a place in his great "Faith's Hall of Fame" in chapter 11, but he sees Enoch from a slightly different perspective. He describes him as "one who pleased God." Here, then, are two important clues: Enoch walked with God, and Enoch pleased God. It is evident from these two statements that Enoch's life was centered in God; God was the focal point, the polestar of his very existence.

Enoch walked with God; he enjoyed a relationship with God; and he pleased God. We could accurately say he was devoted to God. This is the meaning of godliness.

JERRY BRIDGES

23

GOD IS *with* US ...
IN *the* HARD TIMES

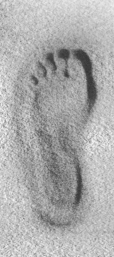

Across the dark sky flashed scenes from my life.

WE ALL GO THROUGH TIMES when life seems to overwhelm us. The Bible reassures us that God's presence is with us to help us, even when we don't realize it.

God is our refuge and strength,
an ever-present help in trouble.

PSALM 46:1

In my distress I called to the LORD,
and he answered me.
From the depths of the grave I called for help,
and you listened to my cry.

JONAH 2:2

The LORD is a refuge for the oppressed,
a stronghold in times of trouble.
Those who know your name will trust in you,
for you, LORD, have never forsaken
those who seek you.

PSALM 9:9–10

You are my hiding place, Lord;
you will protect me from trouble
and surround me with songs of deliverance.

PSALM 32:7

"Do not fear, for I am with you;
do not be dismayed, for I am your God.
I will strengthen you and help you;
I will uphold you with my righteous right hand."

ISAIAH 41:10

The LORD is my strength and my shield;
my heart trusts in him, and I am helped.

PSALM 28:7

Moments of darkness in our lives may be caused by the death of a loved one, the loss of a job or a home or another great tragedy of life. Yet there is a greater darkness than these tragedies: the darkness in the eyes of one who has not felt God's love and grace and the assurance of his hope. There is hope for all of us. There is light. Jesus Christ, the Son of God, is our hope and light in darkness.

You are my lamp, O LORD;
the LORD turns my darkness into light.

2 SAMUEL 22:29

You were once darkness, but now you are light in the
Lord. Live as children of light.

EPHESIANS 5:8

The LORD will be your everlasting light,
and your God will be your glory.

ISAIAH 60:19

You are a chosen people, a royal priesthood, a holy
nation, a people belonging to God, that you may
declare the praises of him who called you out of darkness into his wonderful light.

1 PETER 2:9

In my distress I called to the LORD;
    I called out to my God.
From his temple he heard my voice;
    my cry came to his ears. ...
He reached down from on high and took hold of me;
    he drew me out of deep waters. ...
He brought me out into a spacious place;
    he rescued me because he delighted in me.

2 SAMUEL 22:7, 17, 20

Let him who walks in the dark,
    who has no light,
trust in the name of the LORD
    and rely on his God.

ISAIAH 50:10

The people walking in darkness
    have seen a great light;
on those living in the land of the shadow of death
    a light has dawned.

ISAIAH 9:2

As Paul [my husband, a victim of child abuse who served time in prison as a juvenile offender] read the poem "Footprints," he understood what I was talking about, and he asked if he could read it at the evening retreat service. His message to the young people was that God is always there for us, that, though unseen, He is with us to care for us and carry us through. ... "We can't see Jesus, but He guarantees in His Word that while we were yet sinners He died for us. That's His guarantee. You can't see Him, but He's there ... believe that! There were many times when I seemed to be in utter darkness and I couldn't see Him. I was flailing and lashing out, and sometimes I didn't think He could still love me, but always He was there, carrying me. And that's what He will do for you too."

MARGARET FISHBACK POWERS

Jesus said, "I am the light of the world. Whoever follows me will never walk in darkness, but will have the light of life."

JOHN 8:12

Though I have fallen, I will rise.
Though I sit in darkness,
    the LORD will be my light. ...
He will bring me out into the light;
    I will see his righteousness.

MICAH 7:8–9

Our dark times may also be a time when God wants to teach us something more about ourselves and his love for us. Our faith can be strengthened if we will wait patiently and trust God's heart-desire to make us more like himself.

We are hard pressed on every side, but not crushed; perplexed, but not in despair; persecuted, but not abandoned; struck down, but not destroyed. …We who are alive are always being given over to death for Jesus' sake, so that his life may be revealed in our mortal body.

2 Corinthians 4:8–9, 11

We must go through many hardships to enter the kingdom of God.

Acts 14:22

*A righteous man may have many troubles,
    but the Lord delivers him from them all.*

Psalm 34:19

Our light and momentary troubles are achieving for us an eternal glory that far outweighs them all.

2 Corinthians 4:17

Be joyful in hope, patient in affliction, faithful in prayer.

Romans 12:12

Do not be surprised at the painful trial you are suffering, as though something strange were happening to you. But rejoice that you participate in the sufferings of Christ, so that you may be overjoyed when his glory is revealed.

1 PETER 4:12–13

Tragedy or testing, dark days or dreary nights, God knows what we are facing. He is in touch with what is happening to us, and he is concerned.

God's eyes are on the ways of men;
he sees their every step.

JOB 34:21

The righteous cry out, and the LORD hears them;
he delivers them from all their troubles.
The LORD is close to the brokenhearted
and saves those who are crushed in spirit.

PSALM 34:17–18

Though I walk in the midst of trouble,
you preserve my life ...
with your right hand you save me, Lord.

PSALM 138:7

God knows the way that I take;
when he has tested me, I will come forth as gold.

JOB 23:10

You are the God who sees me.

GENESIS 16:13

I will be glad and rejoice in your love, Lord,
    for you saw my affliction
        and knew the anguish of my soul.

PSALM 31:7

The Lord said, "I have indeed seen the misery of my people. … I have heard them crying out … and I am concerned about their suffering."

EXODUS 3:7

The eyes of the LORD are on the righteous
    and his ears are attentive to their cry.

PSALM 34:15

If anyone had a valid reason to be disappointed in God, it was Joseph, whose valiant stabs at goodness brought him nothing but trouble. He interpreted a dream to his brothers, and they threw him in a cistern. [While] in an Egyptian prison, he interpreted another dream to save a cellmate's life, and the cellmate promptly forgot about him. Through all his trials, Joseph learned to trust: not that God would prevent hardship, but that he would redeem even the hardship. Choking back tears, Joseph tried to explain his faith to his murderous brothers: "You intended to harm me, but God intended it for good …" (Genesis 50:20).

PHILIP YANCEY

GOD IS *with* US ...
As OUR COMPANION

For each scene, I noticed
two sets of footprints in the sand,
one belonging to me and one to my Lord.

ONE OF THE MANY NAMES given to Jesus Christ in the Bible is Emmanuel, which means, literally, "God with us." What a promise is contained in that name! In Christ, God made His dwelling place with ordinary human beings, and as He was returning to heaven, Jesus gave His disciples another great promise, "I am with you always, to the very end of the age." That God is there for us whenever we turn to Him is no pipe-dream!

MARGARET FISHBACK POWERS

"I will walk among you and be your God, and you will be my people."

LEVITICUS 26:12

Blessed are those who have learned to acclaim you, who walk in the light of your presence, O LORD.

PSALM 89:15

We are the temple of the living God. As God has said: "I will live with them and walk among them, and I will be their God, and they will be my people."

2 CORINTHIANS 6:16

The Lord said, "If you do whatever I command you and walk in my ways and do what is right in my eyes by keeping my statutes and commands … I will be with you."

1 KINGS 11:38

The LORD said, "My Presence will go with you, and I will give you rest."

EXODUS 33:14

The Word became flesh and made his dwelling among us. We have seen his glory, the glory of the One and Only, who came from the Father, full of grace and truth.

JOHN 1:14

You have made known to me the path of life, Lord,
you will fill me with joy in your presence,
with eternal pleasures at your right hand.

PSALM 16:11

Two are better than one,
because they have a good return for their work:
If one falls down,
his friend can help him up.
But pity the man who falls
and has no one to help him up!

ECCLESIASTES 4:9–10

Jesus said, "I will ask the Father, and he will give you another Counselor to be with you forever—the Spirit of truth. The world cannot accept him, because it neither sees him nor knows him. But you know him, for he lives with you and will be in you."

JOHN 14:16–17

So many people are of the opinion that because God is an infinite being he is beyond our human comprehension. They have the notion he is someone distant, far removed from us, who may be appealed to only in great extremity across spans of space.

The truth is just the opposite. He is our Father, our Friend, and can be our Companion on the path of life. Such an association becomes the most cherished relationship in the world. But it can only become such if we begin to understand God's character and the wondrous ways in which he deals with us.

W. PHILLIP KELLER

Jesus said, "Here I am! I stand at the door and knock. If anyone hears my voice and opens the door, I will come in and eat with him, and he with me."

REVELATION 3:20

"Abraham believed God, and it was credited to him as righteousness," and he was called God's friend.

JAMES 2:23

Jesus said, "You are my friends if you do what I command.…. I have called you friends, for everything that I learned from my Father I have made known to you. You did not choose me, but I chose you."

JOHN 15:14–16

Wherever we go, we cannot step outside the boundaries of God's love and care. We can have fellowship "with the Father and with his Son, Jesus Christ" wherever we are (1 John 1:3). All we need to do is trust in God's loving companionship and walk the path he has placed before us.

Where can I go from your Spirit?
Where can I flee from your presence?
If I go up to the heavens, you are there;
if I make my bed in the depths, you are there.
If I rise on the wings of the dawn,
if I settle on the far side of the sea,
even there your hand will guide me,
your right hand will hold me fast.

PSALM 139:7–10

"*Where two or three come together in my name, there am I with them*," Jesus said.

MATTHEW 18:20

You have granted him eternal blessings, Lord,
and made him glad with the joy of your presence.

PSALM 21:6

Better is one day in your courts
than a thousand elsewhere;
I would rather be a doorkeeper in the
house of my God
than dwell in the tents of the wicked.

PSALM 84:10

Come, let us return to the LORD.
He has torn us to pieces
  but he will heal us;
he has injured us
  but he will bind up our wounds.
After two days he will revive us;
  on the third day he will restore us,
  that we may live in his presence.

HOSEA 6:1–2

Blessed are those you choose
  and bring near to live in your courts!
We are filled with the good things of your house, Lord,
  of your holy temple.

PSALM 65:4

Since we have confidence to enter the Most Holy
Place by the blood of Jesus, by a new and living way
opened for us through the curtain, that is, his body,
and since we have a great priest over the house of
God, let us draw near to God with a sincere heart in
full assurance of faith.

HEBREWS 10:19–22

May the grace of the Lord Jesus Christ, and the love
of God, and the fellowship of the Holy Spirit be with
you all.

2 CORINTHIANS 13:14

The spiritual giants of old were men who at some time became acutely conscious of the real Presence of God and maintained that consciousness for the rest of their lives.

The first encounter may have been one of terror, as when a "thick and dreadful darkness" came over Abram (Genesis 15:12), or as when Moses at the bush hid his face because he was afraid to look upon God. Usually this fear soon lost its content of terror and changed after a while to delightsome awe, to level off finally into a reverent sense of complete nearness to God. The essential point is this: these were men who experienced God!

How otherwise can the saints and prophets be explained? How otherwise can we account for the amazing power for good they have exercised over countless generations? Is it not that they walked in conscious communion with the real Presence and addressed their prayers to God with the artless conviction that they were addressing Someone actually there?

A. W. TOZER

Surely goodness and love will follow me
  all the days of my life,
and I will dwell in the house of the LORD
  forever.

PSALM 23:6

GOD IS *with* US ...

GIVING OUR LIVES MEANING AND PURPOSE

When the last scene of my life shot before me
I looked back at the footprints in the sand.

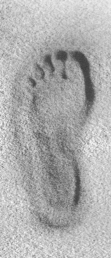

I WENT TO MASS EVERY DAY, I said my prayers, and I tried to live by the Golden Rule.

[But] what I really had was a tiny taste of success and a tiny taste of religion—but not much Christianity. Sure, I was a good person. I treated others with respect. But someone once described the contrast between a good life and a godly life as the difference between the top of the ocean and the bottom. On top, sometimes it's like glass—serene and calm—and other times it's raging and stormy. But hundreds of fathoms below, it is beautiful and consistent, always calm, always peaceful. Down deep in my heart, I did not have the peace that comes only from knowing Jesus Christ as a personal Savior. Back then in 1970, when I was twenty-nine years old and a head football coach for the first time in my life, I was a church-goer and a professing Christian. But it wasn't until four years later, when I was a rookie assistant coach at the University of Michigan that I discovered a real relationship with Jesus Christ. And when I accepted Christ as Savior and Lord of my life, I began an adventure that has transformed my life.

BILL MCCARTNEY

Do not conform any longer to the pattern of this world, but be transformed by the renewing of your mind. Then you will be able to test and approve what God's will is—his good, pleasing and perfect will.

ROMANS 12:2

If anyone is in Christ, he is a new creation; the old has gone, the new has come!

2 CORINTHIANS 5:17

The world and its desires pass away, but the man who does the will of God lives forever.

1 JOHN 2:17

Forgetting what is behind and straining toward what is ahead, I press on toward the goal to win the prize for which God has called me heavenward in Christ Jesus.

PHILIPPIANS 3:13−14

Let us throw off everything that hinders and the sin that so easily entangles, and let us run with perseverance the race marked out for us. Let us fix our eyes on Jesus, the author and perfecter of our faith.

HEBREWS 12:1−2

Run in such a way as to get the prize. Everyone who competes in the games goes into strict training. They do it to get a crown that will not last; but we do it to get a crown that will last forever.

1 CORINTHIANS 9:24−25

I have fought the good fight, I have finished the race, I have kept the faith. Now there is in store for me the crown of righteousness, which the Lord, the righteous Judge, will award to me on that day—and not only to me, but also to all who have longed for his appearing.

2 TIMOTHY 4:7–8

"Forget the former things;
do not dwell on the past.
See, I am doing a new thing!
Now it springs up; do you not perceive it?
I am making a way in the desert
and streams in the wasteland," says the LORD.

ISAIAH 43:18–19

By faith Moses, when he had grown up, refused to be known as the son of Pharaoh's daughter. He chose to be mistreated along with the people of God rather than to enjoy the pleasures of sin for a short time. He regarded disgrace for the sake of Christ as of greater value than the treasures of Egypt, because he was looking ahead to his reward.

HEBREWS 11:24–26

Jesus said, "What good is it for a man to gain the whole world, yet forfeit his soul?"

MARK 8:36

We fix our eyes not on what is seen, but on what is unseen. For what is seen is temporary, but what is unseen is eternal.

2 CORINTHIANS 4:18

I consider everything a loss compared to the surpassing greatness of knowing Christ Jesus my Lord, for whose sake I have lost all things. I consider them rubbish, that I may gain Christ and be found in him.

PHILIPPIANS 3:8–9

[God] perceives clearly why I think as I do; why I feel as I do in interaction with others; why I make the choices I do from day to day. In all these complex activities, he does not come to condemn me. He comes instead to change and re-direct my energies, my decisions, into noble purposes and lofty service. Bless his Name!

W. PHILLIP KELLER

In a large house there are articles not only of gold and silver, but also of wood and clay; some are for noble purposes and some for ignoble. If a man cleanses himself from the latter, he will be an instrument for noble purposes, made holy, useful to the Master and prepared to do any good work.

2 TIMOTHY 2:20–21

Whether you eat or drink or whatever you do, do it all for the glory of God.

1 CORINTHIANS 10:31

Serve wholeheartedly, as if you were serving the Lord, not men, because you know that the Lord will reward everyone for whatever good he does.

EPHESIANS 6:7–8

Offer yourselves to God, as those who have been brought from death to life; and offer the parts of your body to him as instruments of righteousness.

ROMANS 6:13

May the favor of the Lord our God rest upon us;
establish the work of our hands for us—
yes, establish the work of our hands.

PSALM 90:17

Whatever you do, work at it with all your heart, as working for the Lord, not for men, since you know that you will receive an inheritance from the Lord as a reward. It is the Lord Christ you are serving.

COLOSSIANS 3:23–24

No one can lay any foundation other than the one already laid, which is Jesus Christ. If any man builds on this foundation using gold, silver, costly stones, wood, hay or straw, his work will be shown for what it is, because the Day will bring it to light. It will be revealed with fire, and the fire will test the quality of each man's work. If what he has built survives, he will receive his reward.

1 CORINTHIANS 3:11–14

Jesus said, "Do not store up for yourselves treasures on earth, where moth and rust destroy, and where thieves break in and steal. But store up for yourselves treasures in heaven, where moth and rust do not destroy, and where thieves do not break in and steal. For where your treasure is, there your heart will be also."

MATTHEW 6:19–21

Command those who are rich in this present world not to be arrogant nor to put their hope in wealth, which is so uncertain, but to put their hope in God, who richly provides us with everything for our enjoyment. Command them to do good, to be rich in good deeds, and to be generous and willing to share. In this way they will lay up treasure for themselves as a firm foundation for the coming age, so that they may take hold of the life that is truly life.

1 TIMOTHY 6:17–19

Jesus said, "I have come that they may have life, and have it to the full."

JOHN 10:10

God who began a good work in you will carry it on to completion until the day of Christ Jesus.

PHILIPPIANS 1:6

My purpose is that they may be encouraged in heart and united in love, so that they may have the full riches of complete understanding, in order that they may know the mystery of God, namely, Christ, in whom are hidden all the treasures of wisdom and knowledge.

COLOSSIANS 2:2–3

When we have experienced God's forgiveness, we are new creatures. We do not need to live a life of regrets, but rather we can live with a forward-looking hope of glory!

GOD IS *with* US ...

WHEN WE SEEM TO BE ALONE

And to my surprise, I noticed that many times along the path of my life there was only one set of footprints.

I BEGAN TO RECOGNIZE THAT I needed to trust God fully with the events that came into my life. Today I can confidently say that I know that anyone who does that can be sure that God is ordering not only our steps, but also our stops. And even when we feel we are walking a lonely, difficult, or sad path, we are not alone.

MARGARET FISHBACK POWERS

Jesus said, "A time is coming, and has come, when you will be scattered, each to his own home. You will leave me all alone. Yet I am not alone, for my Father is with me."

JOHN 16:32

Do not hide your face from me,
 do not turn your servant away in anger;
 you have been my helper.
Do not reject me or forsake me,
 O God my Savior.

PSALM 27:9

I say to God my Rock,
 "Why have you forgotten me?
Why must I go about mourning,
 oppressed by the enemy?"

PSALM 42:9

My God, my God, why have you forsaken me?
 Why are you so far from saving me,
 so far from the words of my groaning?

PSALM 22:1

When we feel alone and abandoned, we can take comfort in God's promises to deliver us from our isolation and pain.

"He will call upon me, and I will answer him;
I will be with him in trouble,
I will deliver him and honor him.
With long life will I satisfy him
and show him my salvation," says the Lord.

PSALM 91:15–16

"I the LORD will answer them;
I, the God of Israel, will not forsake them."

ISAIAH 41:17

"Can a mother forget the baby at her breast
and have no compassion on the child she has
borne?
Though she may forget,
I will not forget you!
See, I have engraved you on the palms of my
hands," declares the Lord.

ISAIAH 49:15–16

You are enthroned as the Holy One;
you are the praise of Israel.
In you our fathers put their trust;
they trusted and you delivered them.
They cried to you and were saved;
in you they trusted and were not disappointed.

PSALM 22:3–5

Though it appeared God had abandoned him, Job clung to the assurance that *God is who he is.* ...

This is real faith: believing and acting obediently regardless of circumstances or contrary evidence. After all, if faith depended on visible evidence, it wouldn't be faith.

CHARLES COLSON

For the sake of his great name, the LORD will not reject his people, because the Lord was pleased to make you his own.

1 SAMUEL 12:22

Jesus said, "Do not let your hearts be troubled. Trust in God; trust also in me."

JOHN 14:1

"I will be with you; I will never leave you nor forsake you," says the Lord.

JOSHUA 1:5

Jesus said, "I will not leave you as orphans; I will come to you."

JOHN 14:18

God has said,
> *"Never will I leave you;*
> *never will I forsake you."*

HEBREWS 13:5

God is always with us—in our joy and in our pain, in the good times and in the bad times. His steadfast love and faithfulness are promises we can cling to, promises to bring us joy when we face loneliness.

Jesus said, "Surely I am with you always, to the very end of the age."

MATTHEW 28:20

The LORD your God is a merciful God; he will not abandon or destroy you.

DEUTERONOMY 4:31

Be strong and courageous. Do not be afraid or terri-fied, ... for the LORD your God goes with you; he will never leave you nor forsake you.

DEUTERONOMY 31:6

Come near to God and he will come near to you.

JAMES 4:8

The LORD is with you when you are with him. If you seek him, he will be found by you.

2 CHRONICLES 15:2

Why are you downcast, O my soul?
Why so disturbed within me?
Put your hope in God,
for I will yet praise him,
my Savior and my God.

PSALM 42:11

When loneliness overtakes us, we need to remember that we are not alone. God has promised to be with us. He will never forsake us. Lean on his promises and receive his peace.

You know with all your heart and soul that not one of all the good promises the LORD your God gave you has failed. Every promise has been fulfilled; not one has failed.

JOSHUA 23:14

David said about the Lord:
  "I saw the Lord always before me.
  Because he is at my right hand,
  I will not be shaken."

ACTS 2:25

Jesus said, "Whoever has my commands and obeys them, he is the one who loves me. He who loves me will be loved by my Father, and I too will love him and show myself to him."

JOHN 14:21

I pray that you, being rooted and established in love, may have power, together with all the saints, to grasp how wide and long and high and deep is the love of Christ, and to know this love that surpasses knowledge—that you may be filled to the measure of all the fullness of God.

EPHESIANS 3:17–19

Who shall separate us from the love of Christ? Shall trouble or hardship or persecution or famine or nakedness or danger or sword? … No, in all these things we are more than conquerors through him who loved us. For I am convinced that neither death nor life, neither angels nor demons, neither the present nor the future, nor any powers, neither height nor depth, nor anything else in all creation, will be able to separate us from the love of God that is in Christ Jesus our Lord.

ROMANS 8:35, 37–39

It's easy to see God in the miraculous. It's not so easy to see him in the mundane. But that's where most of us live. We live without seeing handwriting on the wall or hearing thunder from Sinai. We live with God not centerstage but directing unobtrusively from the wings.

This is all the more reason why we need to be sensitive to his voice—so we can be aware of and attentive to the subtle ways in which he works.

CHARLES SWINDOLL

GOD IS *with* US ...
IN OUR GRIEF

I realized that this was at the lowest and saddest times of my life.

WHETHER WE FACE DEATH, discouragement, loss or pain, we can take great comfort in knowing that no sorrow is too deep that God cannot feel it with us. And God wants to help deliver us from it. He wants to bring us his divine comfort.

When I said, "My foot is slipping,"
your love, O LORD, supported me.
When anxiety was great within me,
your consolation brought joy to my soul.

PSALM 94:18–19

The LORD upholds all those who fall
and lifts up all who are bowed down.

PSALM 145:14

I sought the LORD, and he answered me;
he delivered me from all my fears.

PSALM 34:4

Jesus said, "Peace I leave with you; my peace I give
you. I do not give to you as the world gives. Do not
let your hearts be troubled and do not be afraid."

JOHN 14:27

Jesus said, "My grace is sufficient for you, for my power
is made perfect in weakness."

2 CORINTHIANS 12:9

We who have fled to take hold of the hope offered to us may be greatly encouraged. We have this hope as an anchor for the soul, firm and secure.

HEBREWS 6:18–19

Praise be to the God and Father of our Lord Jesus Christ, the Father of compassion and the God of all comfort, who comforts us in all our troubles, so that we can comfort those in any trouble with the comfort we ourselves have received from God.

2 CORINTHIANS 1:3–4

God has sent me to bind up the brokenhearted …
to comfort all who mourn,
and provide for those who grieve …
to bestow on them a crown of beauty
instead of ashes,
the oil of gladness
instead of mourning,
and a garment of praise
instead of a spirit of despair.

ISAIAH 61:1–3

My comfort in my suffering is this:
Your promise preserves my life, Lord.

PSALM 119:50

We do not have a high priest who is unable to sympathize with our weaknesses. … Let us then approach the throne of grace with confidence, so that we may receive mercy and find grace to help us in our time of need.

HEBREWS 4:15–16

Jesus experienced sorrow of the deepest kind in the Garden of Gethsemane—the sorrow of impending death. We also experience pain when death takes a loved one, but God reminds us that he is still in control. Death is not the master— God is.

None of us lives to himself alone and none of us dies to himself alone. If we live, we live to the Lord; and if we die, we die to the Lord. So, whether we live or die, we belong to the Lord.

ROMANS 14:7–8

If only for this life we have hope in Christ, we are to be pitied more than all men. But Christ has indeed been raised from the dead. … Since death came through a man, the resurrection of the dead comes also through a man. For as in Adam all die, so in Christ all will be made alive.

1 CORINTHIANS 15:19–22

Listen, I tell you a mystery: We will not all sleep, but we will all be changed—in a flash, in the twinkling of an eye, at the last trumpet. For the trumpet will sound, the dead will be raised imperishable, and we will be changed.

1 CORINTHIANS 15:51–52

We believe that God will bring with Jesus those who have fallen asleep in him. ... For the Lord himself will come down from heaven, with a loud command, with the voice of the archangel and with the trumpet call of God, and the dead in Christ will rise first. After that, we who are still alive and are left will be caught up together with them in the clouds to meet the Lord in the air. And so we will be with the Lord forever.

1 THESSALONIANS 4:14, 16–17

To me, to live is Christ and to die is gain.

PHILIPPIANS 1:21

Jesus said, "I am the resurrection and the life. He who believes in me will live, even though he dies; and who-ever lives and believes in me will never die."

JOHN 11:25–26

Jesus said, "In my Father's house are many rooms; if it were not so, I would have told you. I am going there to prepare a place for you. And if I go and prepare a place for you, I will come back and take you to be with me that you also may be where I am."

JOHN 14:2–3

Our Savior, Christ Jesus ... has destroyed death and has brought life and immortality to light through the gospel.

2 TIMOTHY 1:10

No trial is so great that God cannot deliver us. No pain is so great that he does not bring us comfort. And no situation is ever without God's presence.

"I am the LORD, your God,
*   who takes hold of your right hand*
and says to you, Do not fear;
*   I will help you."*

ISAIAH 41:13

In all their distress the Savior too was distressed,
*   and the angel of his presence saved them.*
In his love and mercy he redeemed them;
*   he lifted them up and carried them.*

ISAIAH 63:9

Though the Lord brings grief, he will show compassion,
*   so great is his unfailing love.*

LAMENTATIONS 3:32

Jesus said, "Come to me, all you who are weary and burdened, and I will give you rest. Take my yoke upon you and learn from me, for I am gentle and humble in heart, and you will find rest for your souls."

MATTHEW 11:28–29

"I will refresh the weary and satisfy the faint," says the Lord.

JEREMIAH 31:25

I love you, O LORD, my strength.
The LORD is my rock, my fortress and my deliverer;
  my God is my rock, in whom I take refuge.
  He is my shield and the horn of my salvation,
    my stronghold.

PSALM 18:1–2

Surely, O LORD, you bless the righteous;
  you surround them with your favor as with a
    shield.

PSALM 5:12

"As a mother comforts her child,
  so will I comfort you," says the LORD.

ISAIAH 66:13

"I will turn their mourning into gladness;
  I will give them comfort and joy instead of sorrow,"
    says the Lord.

JEREMIAH 31:13

You turned my wailing into dancing;
  you removed my sackcloth and clothed me with joy,
that my heart may sing to you and not be silent.
  O LORD my God, I will give you thanks forever.

PSALM 30:11–12

*God will wipe every tear from their eyes. There will be
no more death or mourning or crying or pain.*

REVELATION 21:4

Shout for joy, O heavens;
    rejoice, O earth;
    burst into song, O mountains!
For the LORD comforts his people
    and will have compassion on his afflicted ones.

ISAIAH 49:13

Oh, yes, we mourn ... but we have hope—
bright hope for tomorrow, when all who trust in
Jesus Christ as Savior will move beyond pain and
grief forever because we shall be forever with the
Lord. And it is not just some pipe dream, some
opium to stupefy and mislead hurting people. It
is real, because Christ is real, because in our past
there is a blood-stained cross on which the
Prince of Glory died. Because of that ... we have
hope when all things are made new and death
shall be no more, nor grief, nor crying.

GERALD OOSTERVEEN

GOD IS *with* US ...

ALLAYING OUR CONCERNS

This always bothered me ...

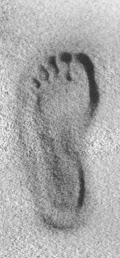

EVEN WHEN WE ARE SURROUNDED by family and friends, some problems seem to double in size of their own accord. If we toss and turn in the early morning hours thinking about them, they become ten times as large. Yet though it seems the whole world has gone wrong around us, we are not alone—God is with us!

Do not fret because of evil men
or be envious of those who do wrong;
for like the grass they will soon wither,
like green plants they will soon die away.
Trust in the LORD and do good.

PSALM 37:1–3

Be still before the LORD and wait patiently for him.

PSALM 37:7

Do not be afraid or discouraged, for the LORD God, my God, is with you. He will not fail you or forsake you.

1 CHRONICLES 28:20

Cast all your anxiety on him because God cares for you.

1 PETER 5:7

Jesus said, "Do not worry about your life, what you will eat; or about your body, what you will wear. Life is more than food, and the body more than clothes."

LUKE 12:22–23

Jesus said, "I have told you these things, so that in me you may have peace. In this world you will have trouble. But take heart! I have overcome the world."

JOHN 16:33

I will say of the LORD, "He is my refuge and my fortress,
my God, in whom I trust."

PSALM 91:2

How great is your goodness, O LORD,
which you have stored up for those who fear you,
which you bestow in the sight of men
on those who take refuge in you.
In the shelter of your presence you hide them ...
in your dwelling you keep them safe.

PSALM 31:19–20

God shielded him and cared for him;
he guarded him as the apple of his eye,
like an eagle that stirs up its nest
and hovers over its young,
that spreads its wings to catch them
and carries them on its pinions.

DEUTERONOMY 32:10–11

Everyone born of God overcomes the world. This is the victory that has overcome the world, even our faith. Who is it that overcomes the world? Only he who believes that Jesus is the Son of God.

1 JOHN 5:4–5

Worry casts a big shadow over small problems—
a shadow that should never cross our lives.

Those who trust in the LORD are like Mount Zion,
which cannot be shaken but endures forever.

PSALM 125:1

Jesus said, "Who of you by worrying can add a single
hour to his life? And why do you worry about clothes?
See how the lilies of the field grow. They do not labor
or spin. Yet I tell you that not even Solomon in all his
splendor was dressed like one of these. If that is how
God clothes the grass of the field, which is here today
and tomorrow is thrown into the fire, will he not much
more clothe you, O you of little faith?"

MATTHEW 6:27–30

The LORD is close to the brokenhearted
and saves those who are crushed in spirit.
A righteous man may have many troubles,
but the LORD delivers him from them all.

PSALM 34:18–19

Even though I walk
through the valley of the shadow of death,
I will fear no evil,
for you are with me, Lord;
your rod and your staff,
they comfort me.

PSALM 23:4

"I am concerned for you and will look on you with favor," says the LORD.

The LORD gives strength to his people;
 the LORD blesses his people with peace.

PSALM 29:11

Jesus said, "My sheep listen to my voice; I know them, and they follow me. I give them eternal life, and they shall never perish; no one can snatch them out of my hand. My Father, who has given them to me, is greater than all; no one can snatch them out of my Father's hand. I and the Father are one."

JOHN 10:27–30

Blessed is the man who trusts in the LORD,
 whose confidence is in him.
He will be like a tree planted by the water
 that sends out its roots by the stream.
It does not fear when heat comes;
 its leaves are always green.
It has no worries in a year of drought
 and never fails to bear fruit.

JEREMIAH 17:7–8

Cast your cares on the LORD
 and he will sustain you;
 he will never let the righteous fall.

PSALM 55:22

This world is filled with threats—some imagined, some real—to our safety, to our sense of being okay. The ultimate security, the only true safety, is to be in right relationship with the God who is the alpha and omega, the beginning and the end. He was there before the beginning. He has no end. He has seen and suffered all. He has known our fears. He sets us free.

DANIEL TAYLOR

Be on your guard; stand firm in the faith; be men of courage; be strong.

1 CORINTHIANS 16:13

He who fears the LORD has a secure fortress, and for his children it will be a refuge.

PROVERBS 14:26

Great peace have they who love your law, Lord, and nothing can make them stumble.

PSALM 119:165

We say with confidence,
    "The Lord is my helper; I will not be afraid. What can man do to me?"

HEBREWS 13:6

The LORD himself goes before you and will be with you; he will never leave you nor forsake you. Do not be afraid; do not be discouraged.

DEUTERONOMY 31:8

Do not be anxious about anything, but in everything, by prayer and petition, with thanksgiving, present your requests to God. And the peace of God, which transcends all understanding, will guard your hearts and your minds in Christ Jesus.

PHILIPPIANS 4:6–7

If you make the Most High your dwelling—
   even the LORD, who is my refuge—
then no harm will befall you,
   no disaster will come near your tent.

PSALM 91:9–10

I will lie down and sleep in peace,
   for you alone, O LORD,
   make me dwell in safety.

PSALM 4:8

I'd like to suggest that the next time you can't sleep, you get up, find a place to kneel in prayer and thank God for what He has done on the cross in love for you! Understand that this Heavenly Father really is caring, compassionate, comforting and concerned. Have faith in His goodness for your life and trust Him with it, then go back to bed and get a good night's rest, secure in the knowledge of His unconditional promises of love for you!

MARGARET FISHBACK POWERS

GOD IS *with* US ...

DIRECTING OUR STEPS

And I questioned the Lord
about my dilemma.

WHEN A TRANSIT STRIKE BROUGHT our recently purchased business to a standstill, I found myself wondering if we had made the right decision to get into this new business. The choice seemed to be the right one at the time, but now I wasn't so sure. How was I supposed to sort out what we should do next? When we face questions of this kind, we need to get our arms around God's wisdom.

"I will instruct you and teach you in the way you
should go;
I will counsel you and watch over you," says the Lord.

PSALM 32:8

Trust in the LORD with all your heart
and lean not on your own understanding;
in all your ways acknowledge him,
and he will make your paths straight.

PROVERBS 3:5-6

The way of a fool seems right to him,
but a wise man listens to advice.

PROVERBS 12:15

The LORD will guide you always;
he will satisfy your needs in a sun-scorched land
and will strengthen your frame.
You will be like a well-watered garden,
like a spring whose waters never fail.

ISAIAH 58:11

Many times along our life-walk the path becomes obscure. We need someone to help show us the way. That someone is God.

Show me the way I should go, Lord,
for to you I lift up my soul.

PSALM 143:8

Show me your ways, O LORD,
teach me your paths;
guide me in your truth and teach me,
for you are God my Savior,
and my hope is in you all day long.

PSALM 25:4–5

God will teach us his ways,
so that we may walk in his paths.

ISAIAH 2:3

The LORD is my shepherd, I shall not be in want.
He makes me lie down in green pastures,
he leads me beside quiet waters,
he restores my soul.
He guides me in paths of righteousness
for his name's sake.

PSALM 23:1–3

Whether you turn to the right or to the left, your ears
will hear a voice behind you, saying, "This is the way;
walk in it."

ISAIAH 30:21

God doesn't mind our questions when we come to him with a seeking heart. God is bigger than any question we can ask. And he often will give us the answers we seek in his Word.

Your word is a lamp to my feet
  and a light for my path, O Lord.

PSALM 119:105

These commands are a lamp,
  this teaching is a light,
and the corrections of discipline
  are the way to life.

PROVERBS 6:23

Do not let this Book of the Law depart from your mouth; meditate on it day and night, so that you may be careful to do everything written in it. Then you will be prosperous and successful.

JOSHUA 1:8

Pay attention and listen to the sayings of the wise;
  apply your heart to what I teach,
for it is pleasing when you keep them in your heart
  and have all of them ready on your lips.

PROVERBS 22:17–18

The law of the LORD is perfect,
reviving the soul.
The statutes of the LORD are trustworthy,
making wise the simple.
The precepts of the LORD are right,
giving joy to the heart.
The commands of the LORD are radiant,
giving light to the eyes. ...
By them is your servant warned;
in keeping them there is great reward.

PSALM 19:7–8, 11

Wisdom is supreme; therefore get wisdom.
Though it cost all you have, get understanding.

PROVERBS 4:7

Blessed is the man who finds wisdom,
the man who gains understanding,
for she is more profitable than silver
and yields better returns than gold.
She is more precious than rubies;
nothing you desire can compare with her.
Long life is in her right hand;
in her left hand are riches and honor.
Her ways are pleasant ways,
and all her paths are peace.
She is a tree of life to those who embrace her;
those who lay hold of her will be blessed.

PROVERBS 3:13–18

As the verse of one of my favorite hymns, "Amazing Grace," reminds us, we have a Guide who accompanies us every step of the way and who will welcome us home at last:

"Through many dangers,
toils and snares,
I have already come;
'tis grace has brought me safe thus far,
and grace will lead me home."

JOHN NEWTON 1725–1807

You are my rock and my fortress, O LORD,
*   for the sake of your name lead and guide me.*

PSALM 31:3

Show me your ways, O LORD,
*   teach me your paths;*
guide me in your truth and teach me,
*   for you are God my Savior,*
*   and my hope is in you all day long.*

PSALM 25:4–5

I guide you in the way of wisdom
*   and lead you along straight paths.*
When you walk, your steps will not be hampered;
*   when you run, you will not stumble.*

PROVERBS 4:11–12

We used to play a game at summer camp in which we would blindfold one of the kids and have him or her run through a wooded area, relying on a friend for verbal directions to help navigate. "Turn to the left; there's a tree coming!" "There's a log in front of you—*jump!*" Some kids would not trust the verbal directions whatsoever. They would shuffle their feet and walk very slowly, even though their friends were shouting that the way was clear. Other kids would trot along, and a few would go like gangbusters. All the kids, though, had to fight the urge to tear off the blindfold so that they could see what was ahead. It takes a great deal of courage to follow another person's lead.

As Christians, we sometimes feel like those blindfolded children. Paul says in 2 Corinthians 5:7, "We live by faith, not by sight." We are not alone in the woods, though—God will direct our paths.

BILL HYBELS

GOD IS *with* US ...

IN OUR DECISIONS

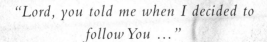

"Lord, you told me when I decided to follow You ..."

WE ALL NEED GOD'S DIVINE power from day to day to follow in his footsteps—to learn the eternal, upside-down, inside-out values of God's kingdom so that we may make decisions based on his character and ultimately share in his glory.

The LORD gives wisdom,
and from his mouth come knowledge and
understanding.

PROVERBS 2:6

Where then does wisdom come from?
Where does understanding dwell?
It is hidden from the eyes of every living thing,
concealed even from the birds of the air. ...
God understands the way to it
and he alone knows where it dwells.

JOB 28:20–21, 23

If any of you lacks wisdom, he should ask God, who
gives generously to all without finding fault, and it will
be given to him.

JAMES 1:5

God is greater than our hearts, and he knows everything.

1 JOHN 3:20

I know whom I have believed, and am convinced that God is able to guard what I have entrusted to him for that day.

2 TIMOTHY 1:12

This is my prayer: that your love may abound more and more in knowledge and depth of insight, so that you may be able to discern what is best and may be pure and blameless until the day of Christ, filled with the fruit of righteousness that comes through Jesus Christ—to the glory and praise of God.

PHILIPPIANS 1:9–11

Jesus said, "My decisions are right, because I am not alone. I stand with the Father, who sent me."

JOHN 8:16

Preserve sound judgment and discernment,
*   do not let them out of your sight;*
they will be life for you,
*   an ornament to grace your neck.*
Then you will go on your way in safety,
*   and your foot will not stumble.*

PROVERBS 3:21–23

The decisions we need to make may be simple or they may be complex, but they should always be predicated on our decision to follow the Lord.

Fear the LORD and serve him faithfully with all your heart; consider what great things he has done for you.

1 SAMUEL 12:24

The LORD is good to those whose hope is in him, to the one who seeks him.

LAMENTATIONS 3:25

Commit to the LORD whatever you do, and your plans will succeed.

PROVERBS 16:3

The integrity of the upright guides them.

PROVERBS 11:3

Choose for yourselves this day whom you will serve. ... As for me and my household, we will serve the LORD.

JOSHUA 24:15

It is the LORD your God you must follow, and him you must revere. Keep his commands and obey him; serve him and hold fast to him.

DEUTERONOMY 13:4

*Those who live according to the sinful nature have
their minds set on what that nature desires; but those
who live in accordance with the Spirit have their minds
set on what the Spirit desires.*

ROMANS 8:5

*A man reaps what he sows. The one who sows to please
his sinful nature, from that nature will reap destruction;
the one who sows to please the Spirit, from the Spirit
will reap eternal life. Let us not become weary in doing
good, for at the proper time we will reap a harvest if
we do not give up. Therefore, as we have opportunity,
let us do good to all people.*

GALATIANS 6:7–10

*The grace of God that brings salvation has appeared
to all men. It teaches us to say "No" to ungodliness
and worldly passions, and to live self-controlled,
upright and godly lives in this present age.*

TITUS 2:11–12

Your commands make me wiser than my enemies,
    O LORD,
    for they are ever with me.
I have more insight than all my teachers,
    for I meditate on your statutes.
I have more understanding than the elders,
    for I obey your precepts.

PSALM 119:98–100

When we decide to follow the Lord, it means we must live our lives the way he wants us to, following his commands, yielded to his control.

God did not call us to be impure, but to live a holy life.

1 THESSALONIANS 4:7

Serve him with wholehearted devotion and with a willing mind, for the LORD searches every heart and understands every motive behind the thoughts.

1 CHRONICLES 28:9

Now that you have been set free from sin and have become slaves to God, the benefit you reap leads to holiness, and the result is eternal life.

ROMANS 6:22

Let us purify ourselves from everything that contaminates body and spirit, perfecting holiness out of reverence for God.

2 CORINTHIANS 7:1

Just as he who called you is holy, so be holy in all you do; for it is written: "Be holy, because I am holy."

1 PETER 1:15–16

Pursue righteousness, godliness, faith, love, endurance and gentleness. Fight the good fight of the faith.

1 TIMOTHY 6:11-12

Do not turn away from the LORD, but serve the LORD with all your heart.

1 SAMUEL 12:20

Let your eyes look straight ahead,
    fix your gaze directly before you.
Make level paths for your feet
    and take only ways that are firm.

PROVERBS 4:25-26

We must pay more careful attention, therefore, to what we have heard, so that we do not drift away.

HEBREWS 2:1

The fruit of the Spirit is love, joy, peace, patience, kindness, goodness, faithfulness, gentleness and self-control. … Since we live by the Spirit, let us keep in step with the Spirit.

GALATIANS 5:22-23, 25

Now all has been heard;
    here is the conclusion of the matter:
Fear God and keep his commandments,
    for this is the whole duty of man.

ECCLESIASTES 12:13

*"He follows my decrees
    and faithfully keeps my laws.
That man is righteous;
    he will surely live,"
    declares the Sovereign LORD.*

 EZEKIEL 18:9

If anyone speaks, he should do it as one speaking the very words of God. If anyone serves, he should do it with the strength God provides, so that in all things God may be praised through Jesus Christ.

1 PETER 4:11

Wisdom isn't a scholastic accomplishment measured by high scores on the College Boards or admission to an Ivy League college. The true test of knowledge, according to Proverbs, goes beyond academic achievement to moral responsibility. It zooms in on decision-making and shows itself best in the disciplining of the character; this results in "a disciplined and prudent life" [Proverbs 1:1–7]. To live prudently means to think clearly about one's choices and arrive at decisions controlled not by whim or appetite but by an understanding of the difference between right and wrong.

D. BRUCE LOCKERBIE

GOD IS *with* US ...

AS OUR TEACHER
AND MENTOR

*"You would walk and talk with me
all the way."*

God walks and talks with us each day, wherever we are, for "this God is our God for ever and ever; he will be our guide even to the end" (Psalm 48:14).

God guides the humble in what is right
and teaches them his way.

PSALM 25:9

Righteousness goes before the Lord
and prepares the way for his steps.

PSALM 85:13

Remember, O LORD, how I have walked before you
faithfully and with wholehearted devotion and have
done what is good in your eyes.

2 KINGS 20:3

You have delivered me from death
and my feet from stumbling,
that I may walk before God
in the light of life.

PSALM 56:13

This is what the LORD says—
your Redeemer, the Holy One of Israel:
"I am the LORD your God,
who teaches you what is best for you,
who directs you in the way you should go."

ISAIAH 48:17

You guide me with your counsel, Lord,
and afterward you will take me into glory.

PSALM 73:24

Teach me your way, O LORD;
lead me in a straight path.

PSALM 27:11

Lead me, O LORD, in your righteousness …
make straight your way before me.

PSALM 5:8

Teach me to do your will,
for you are my God;
may your good Spirit
lead me on level ground.

PSALM 143:10

God who has compassion on them will guide them
and lead them beside springs of water.

ISAIAH 49:10

May the nations be glad and sing for joy,
for you, O God, rule the peoples justly
and guide the nations of the earth.

PSALM 67:4

God is exalted in his power.
  Who is a teacher like him?
Who has prescribed his ways for him,
  or said to him, 'You have done wrong'?
Remember to extol his work,
  which men have praised in song.
All mankind has seen it;
  men gaze on it from afar.
How great is God—beyond our understanding!
  The number of his years is past finding out.

JOB 36:22–26

The Spirit searches all things, even the deep things of God. For who among men knows the thoughts of a man except the man's spirit within him? In the same way no one knows the thoughts of God except the Spirit of God. We have not received the spirit of the world but the Spirit who is from God, that we may understand what God has freely given us. This is what we speak, not in words taught us by human wisdom but in words taught by the Spirit, expressing spiritual truths in spiritual words.

1 CORINTHIANS 2:10–13

[Nicodemus] came to Jesus at night and said, "Rabbi, we know you are a teacher who has come from God. For no one could perform the miraculous signs you are doing if God were not with him."

JOHN 3:2

Only in Jesus, the Son of God, can we truly know God the Father ...

What we think of God makes a tremendous difference in our lives. Where we get our ideas of God makes a tremendous difference too. We can gather up data and develop our own image of God, or we can allow God to reveal himself in a self-portrait—his Son, Jesus Christ.

REUBEN R. WELCH

Jesus took with him Peter, James and John the brother of James, and led them up a high mountain by themselves. There he was transfigured before them. His face shone like the sun, and his clothes became as white as the light. ... A bright cloud enveloped them, and a voice from the cloud said, "This is my Son, whom I love; with him I am well pleased. Listen to him!"

MATTHEW 17:1–2, 5

In the past God spoke to our forefathers through the prophets at many times and in various ways, but in these last days he has spoken to us by his Son, whom he appointed heir of all things, and through whom he made the universe. The Son is the radiance of God's glory and the exact representation of his being, sustaining all things by his powerful word.

HEBREWS 1:1–3

When the Sabbath came, Jesus went into the synagogue and began to teach. The people were amazed at his teaching, because he taught them as one who had authority, not as the teachers of the law.

MARK 1:21–22

An expert in the law tested Jesus with this question: "Teacher, which is the greatest commandment in the Law?"
Jesus replied: "'Love the Lord your God with all your heart and with all your soul and with all your mind.' This is the first and greatest commandment. And the second is like it: 'Love your neighbor as yourself.' All the Law and the Prophets hang on these two commandments."

MATTHEW 22:35–40

Jesus said, "If anyone loves me, he will obey my teaching. My Father will love him, and we will come to him and make our home with him."

JOHN 14:23

Jesus said, "If you hold to my teaching, you are really my disciples. Then you will know the truth, and the truth will set you free."

JOHN 8:31–32

Jesus said, "Anyone who has seen me has seen the Father."

JOHN 14:9

When Jesus had finished washing the disciples' feet, he put on his clothes and returned to his place. "Do you understand what I have done for you?" he asked them. "You call me 'Teacher' and 'Lord,' and rightly so, for that is what I am. Now that I, your Lord and Teacher, have washed your feet, you also should wash one another's feet. I have set you an example that you should do as I have done for you. I tell you the truth, no servant is greater than his master, nor is a messenger greater than the one who sent him. Now that you know these things, you will be blessed if you do them."

JOHN 13:12–17

Your attitude should be the same as that of Christ Jesus:
Who, being in very nature God,
did not consider equality with God something to be grasped,
but made himself nothing,
taking the very nature of a servant.

PHILIPPIANS 2:5–7

Jesus said, "The Counselor, the Holy Spirit, whom the Father will send in my name, will teach you all things and will remind you of everything I have said to you."

JOHN 14:26

Jesus said, "When he, the Spirit of truth, comes, he will guide you into all truth. He will not speak on his own; he will speak only what he hears, and he will tell you what is yet to come. He will bring glory to me by taking from what is mine and making it known to you. All that belongs to the Father is mine. That is why I said the Spirit will take from what is mine and make it known to you."

JOHN 16:13–15

Jesus Christ is God in focus! In him we see God clearly, distinctly, sharply, *down to earth!* ...

If you want to know what God is like, look at his Son. If you want to hear God, listen to his Son! *A man will make no mistake following Christ!*

Let a man begin with Jesus wherever he must to be honest with himself; let him investigate Jesus all the way. Let him go along with Jesus as far as truth dictates—as far as honest inquiry leads.

He will begin to realize that *Jesus is God in focus* ...

You can't go wrong trusting Christ, following Christ, worshiping Christ! He will lead you to a personal, dynamic experience of God.

RICHARD HALVERSON

GOD IS *with* US ...

IN OUR CHALLENGES

"But I'm aware that during the most troublesome times of my life there is only one set of footprints."

WHAT WE NEED TO KNOW, of course, is not just that God exists, not just that beyond the steely brightness of the stars there is a cosmic intelligence of some kind that keeps the whole show going, but that there is a God right here in the thick of our day-by-day lives who may not be writing messages about himself in the stars but in one way or another is trying to get messages through our blindness as we move around here knee-deep in the fragrant muck and misery and marvel of the world. It is not objective proof of God's existence that we want but the experience of God's presence. That is the miracle we are really after, and that is also, I think, the miracle that we really get.

FREDERICK BUECHNER

Therefore we do not lose heart. Though outwardly we are wasting away, yet inwardly we are being renewed day by day. For our light and momentary troubles are achieving for us an eternal glory that far outweighs them all. So we fix our eyes not on what is seen, but on what is unseen. For what is seen is temporary, but what is unseen is eternal.

2 CORINTHIANS 4:16–18

The Lord said, "My grace is sufficient for you, for my power is made perfect in weakness." Therefore I will boast all the more gladly about my weaknesses, so that Christ's power may rest on me. That is why, for Christ's sake, I delight in weaknesses, in insults, in hardships, in persecutions, in difficulties. For when I am weak, then I am strong.

2 CORINTHIANS 12:9–10

Consider it pure joy, my brothers, whenever you face trials of many kinds, because you know that the testing of your faith develops perseverance. Perseverance must finish its work so that you may be mature and complete, not lacking anything.

JAMES 1:2–4

Be strong in the Lord and in his mighty power. Put on the full armor of God so that you can take your stand against the devil's schemes. For our struggle is not against flesh and blood, but against the rulers, against the authorities, against the powers of this dark world and against the spiritual forces of evil in the heavenly realms. Therefore put on the full armor of God, so that … you may be able to stand your ground, and after you have done everything, to stand.

EPHESIANS 6:10–13

We … rejoice in our sufferings, because we know that suffering produces perseverance; perseverance, character; and character, hope. And hope does not disappoint us, because God has poured out his love into our hearts by the Holy Spirit, whom he has given us.

ROMANS 5:3–5

Everything that was written in the past was written to teach us, so that through endurance and the encouragement of the Scriptures we might have hope.

ROMANS 15:4

*Blessed is the man who perseveres under trial, because
when he has stood the test, he will receive the crown
of life that God has promised to those who love him.*

JAMES 1:12

God will never let us down. He promises us his
strength, his peace, his comfort and his presence.
All we need to do is depend on him.

*Put your hope in the LORD,
    for with the LORD is unfailing love
    and with him is full redemption.*

PSALM 130:7

*When I am afraid,
    I will trust in you.
In God, whose word I praise,
    in God I trust; I will not be afraid.*

PSALM 56:3–4

*As for me, I watch in hope for the LORD,
    I wait for God my Savior;
    my God will hear me.*

MICAH 7:7

*Do not be afraid. Stand firm and you will see the deliverance the LORD will bring you today. … The LORD
will fight for you; you need only to be still.*

EXODUS 14:13–14

*The LORD longs to be gracious to you;
    he rises to show you compassion.*

ISAIAH 30:18

The eyes of the LORD range throughout the earth to strengthen those whose hearts are fully committed to him.

2 CHRONICLES 16:9

I wait for you, O LORD;
*   you will answer, O Lord my God.*

PSALM 38:15

You will call, and the LORD will answer;
*   you will cry for help, and he will say: Here am I.*

ISAIAH 58:9

May you be richly rewarded by the LORD, the God of Israel, under whose wings you have come to take refuge.

RUTH 2:12

It is God who arms me with strength
*   and makes my way perfect.*
He makes my feet like the feet of a deer;
*   he enables me to stand on the heights.*
He trains my hands for battle;
*   my arms can bend a bow of bronze.*
You give me your shield of victory,
*   and your right hand sustains me;*
*   you stoop down to make me great.*
You broaden the path beneath me,
*   so that my ankles do not turn.*

PSALM 18:32–36

Those things we consider difficulties are often God's opportunities for our greater blessing. We must trust, believe, hope and continue to walk the path he has laid before us.

Evening, morning and noon
　　I cry out in distress,
　　And God hears my voice.

PSALM 55:17

If the LORD delights in a man's way,
　　he makes his steps firm;
though he stumble, he will not fall,
　　for the LORD upholds him with his hand.

PSALM 37:23–24

The LORD is good,
　　a refuge in times of trouble.
He cares for those who trust in him.

NAHUM 1:7

May our Lord Jesus Christ himself and God our
Father, who loved us and by his grace gave us eternal
encouragement and good hope, encourage your hearts
and strengthen you in every good deed and word.

2 THESSALONIANS 2:16–17

We desperately need to know that Jesus is our brother, with us as we struggle on the way, having the compassion that can only come through his shared experience of suffering and temptation. … He is with us in sympathy and help, not at the end of our struggle, but all the way through.

This is the only way, I believe, that we can maintain vitality and energy and joy in the long haul of the Christian life. Someone has to help us *at the time of our struggle;* we need help *while we are trying;* we need a brother *in the hour of trial,* and especially when we fail. … We need to know that we are known, understood and loved by someone who has marked out the path, has won the victory and is with us on the way. That someone is Jesus.

REUBEN R. WELCH

Yet this I call to mind
and therefore I have hope:
Because of the LORD's great love we are not
consumed,
for his compassions never fail.
They are new every morning;
great is your faithfulness.

LAMENTATIONS 3:21–23

GOD IS *with* US ...

IN OUR CONFUSION

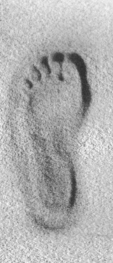

"I just don't understand why, when I needed You most, You leave me."

MANY THINGS IN LIFE CANNOT be explained: the death of an infant, the loss of a job, the rebellion of a child, the desertion by a loved one, or any number of circumstances beyond our control. Have you ever wondered *Why did this have to happen?* God can help us with those "Why?" questions.

Has his unfailing love vanished forever?
  Has his promise failed for all time?
Has God forgotten to be merciful?
  Has he in anger withheld his compassion?

PSALM 77:8–9

The LORD is near to all who call on him,
  to all who call on him in truth.
He fulfills the desires of those who fear him;
  he hears their cry and saves them.

PSALM 145:18–19

Why, O LORD, do you stand far off?
  Why do you hide yourself in times of trouble?

PSALM 10:1

"Call to me and I will answer you and tell you great and unsearchable things you do not know," says the LORD.

JEREMIAH 33:3

The LORD knows the way that I take;
  when he has tested me, I will come forth as gold.

JOB 23:10

There is a time for everything,
    and a season for every activity under heaven.

ECCLESIASTES 3:1

Why do the wicked live on,
    growing old and increasing in power?
They see their children established around them,
    their offspring before their eyes.
Their homes are safe and free from fear;
    the rod of God is not upon them.

JOB 21:7–9

"My thoughts are not your thoughts,
    neither are your ways my ways,"
        declares the LORD.
"As the heavens are higher than the earth,
    so are my ways higher than your ways
    and my thoughts than your thoughts."

ISAIAH 55:8–9

God has not despised or disdained
    the suffering of the afflicted one;
he has not hidden his face from him
    but has listened to his cry for help.

PSALM 22:24

When times are good, be happy;
    but when times are bad, consider:
God has made the one
    as well as the other.

ECCLESIASTES 7:14

Though it may sometimes seem that things are out of control, we can take comfort in God's enduring promises and constant presence.

We know that in all things God works for the good of those who love him, who have been called according to his purpose.

ROMANS 8:28

Let us acknowledge the LORD;
let us press on to acknowledge him.
As surely as the sun rises,
he will appear;
he will come to us like the winter rains,
like the spring rains that water the earth.

HOSEA 6:3

"I will make an everlasting covenant with them: I will never stop doing good to them," says the Lord.

JEREMIAH 32:40

Be strong and courageous. Do not be terrified; do not be discouraged, for the LORD your God will be with you wherever you go.

JOSHUA 1:9

"You will seek me and find me when you seek me with all your heart. I will be found by you," declares the LORD.

JEREMIAH 29:13–14

The LORD is good and his love endures forever;
  his faithfulness continues through all generations.

PSALM 100:5

Our citizenship is in heaven. And we eagerly await a Savior from there, the Lord Jesus Christ, who, by the power that enables him to bring everything under his control, will transform our lowly bodies so that they will be like his glorious body.

PHILIPPIANS 3:20–21

"I am bringing my righteousness near,
  it is not far away;
  and my salvation will not be delayed," says the Lord.

ISAIAH 46:13

Arise, shine, for your light has come,
  and the glory of the LORD rises upon you.
See, darkness covers the earth
  and thick darkness is over the peoples,
but the LORD rises upon you
  and his glory appears over you.

ISAIAH 60:1–2

When we find ourselves questioning God's reason for allowing certain things to happen, we must stop, remember God's faithfulness and depend upon his grace. Whatever our questions, whatever our circumstances, God is still in control.

You, O Lord, are a compassionate and gracious God,
slow to anger, abounding in love and faithfulness.

PSALM 86:15

Who is a God like you,
who pardons sin and forgives the transgression
of the remnant of his inheritance?
You do not stay angry forever
but delight to show mercy.
You will again have compassion on us.

MICAH 7:18–19

Let us hold unswervingly to the hope we profess, for God who promised is faithful.

HEBREWS 10:23

God, who has called you into fellowship with his Son Jesus Christ our Lord, is faithful.

1 CORINTHIANS 1:9

"Blessed are you who hunger now,
  for you will be satisfied.
Blessed are you who weep now,
  for you will laugh."

LUKE 6:21

Six years ago our daughter was involved in a serious accident and many were the times when I have felt great concern over her physical, emotional and spiritual health. But whenever I hit rock-bottom, I would be overwhelmed by a tangible sense of God's love and care. It felt like a warm wave washing over me, and His voice would come to me in a whisper, "I love you and will never leave you." As He breathed encouragement to me, I, in turn, was able to breathe encouragement that gave her strength to try to do things that she felt were not possible. ...

Against all the odds, we have seen our daughter's shattered hopes and ambitions rise to new life. This same overwhelming and powerful love raised Jesus from the dead and today it can bring resurrection joy to your heart.

The way is dark, Heavenly Father, cloud upon cloud is gathering thickly about my head. Lord, thunder roars above me; Father, I stand like one bewildered! Dear Father, take my hand and through the gloom lead safely home Thy child.

GOD IS *with* US ...

AS OUR LOVING FATHER

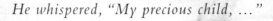

He whispered, "My precious child, ..."

THE CREATOR OF THE UNIVERSE calls me his child—what a blessing! What a privilege! What a responsibility!

"I will be a Father to you,
and you will be my sons and daughters,
*   says the Lord Almighty."*

2 CORINTHIANS 6:18

You are my Father,
*   my God, the Rock my Savior.*

PSALM 89:26

The LORD disciplines those he loves,
*   as a father the son he delights in.*

PROVERBS 3:12

Endure hardship as discipline; God is treating you as
sons. For what son is not disciplined by his father?

HEBREWS 12:7

To us a child is born,
*   to us a son is given,*
*   and the government will be on his shoulders.*
And he will be called ...
*   Everlasting Father.*

ISAIAH 9:6

You, O LORD, are our Father,
our Redeemer from of old is your name.

ISAIAH 63:16

O LORD, you are our Father.
We are the clay, you are the potter;
we are all the work of your hand.

ISAIAH 64:8

You did not receive a spirit that makes you a slave
again to fear, but you received the Spirit of sonship.
And by him we cry, "Abba, Father."

ROMANS 8:15

There is one body and one Spirit—just as you were
called to one hope when you were called—one Lord,
one faith, one baptism; one God and Father of all,
who is over all and through all and in all.

EPHESIANS 4:4–6

How great is the love the Father has lavished on us,
that we should be called children of God! And that
is what we are!

1 JOHN 3:1

As children of God we can trust that our Father will provide for us.

Jesus said, "Which of you fathers, if your son asks for a fish, will give him a snake instead? Or if he asks for an egg, will give him a scorpion? If you then, though you are evil, know how to give good gifts to your children, how much more will your Father in heaven give the Holy Spirit to those who ask him!"

LUKE 11:11–13

Jesus said, "I tell you, do not worry about your life, what you will eat or drink; or about your body, what you will wear. Is not life more important than food, and the body more important than clothes? Look at the birds of the air; they do not sow or reap or store away in barns, and yet your heavenly Father feeds them. Are you not much more valuable than they? … So do not worry, saying, 'What shall we eat?' or 'What shall we drink?' or 'What shall we wear?' For the pagans run after all these things, and your heavenly Father knows that you need them."

MATTHEW 6:25–26, 31–32

The Israelites asked, and God brought them quail
and satisfied them with the bread of heaven.
He opened the rock, and water gushed out;
like a river it flowed in the desert.

PSALM 105:40–41

Jesus said, "Your Father knows what you need before you ask him. This, then, is how you should pray:

"'Our Father in heaven,
hallowed be your name,
your kingdom come,
your will be done
    on earth as it is in heaven.
Give us today our daily bread.
Forgive us our debts,
    as we also have forgiven our debtors.
And lead us not into temptation,
but deliver us from the evil one.'"

MATTHEW 6:8–13

God has shown kindness by giving you rain from heaven and crops in their seasons; he provides you with plenty of food and fills your hearts with joy.

ACTS 14:17

"My people will be filled with my bounty,"
    declares the LORD.

JEREMIAH 31:14

Our loving Father cares for us as a shepherd cares for his sheep. And we, his children, need to listen carefully to his voice and obey.

Jesus said, "The sheep listen to [the Shepherd's] voice. He calls his own sheep by name and leads them out. When he has brought out all his own, he goes on ahead of them, and his sheep follow him because they know his voice."

JOHN 10:3–4

God tends his flock like a shepherd:
He gathers the lambs in his arms
and carries them close to his heart;
he gently leads those that have young.

ISAIAH 40:11

Listen, listen to me, and eat what is good,
and your soul will delight in the richest of fare.

ISAIAH 55:2

Jesus said, "I am the good shepherd; I know my sheep and my sheep know me—just as the Father knows me and I know the Father—and I lay down my life for the sheep."

JOHN 10:14–15

Save your people and bless your inheritance,
O LORD;
be their shepherd and carry them forever.

PSALM 28:9

Scripture repeatedly presents God's desire to be personally and intimately involved with his children. He wants to provide the warmth, affection, discipline and accountability that characterize a parent's loving relationship.

BILL HYBELS

This is what the LORD says …
  he who formed you …
"Fear not, for I have redeemed you;
  I have summoned you by name; you are mine."

ISAIAH 43:1

Praise be to the God and Father of our Lord Jesus Christ, who has blessed us in the heavenly realms with every spiritual blessing in Christ. For he chose us in him before the creation of the world to be holy and blameless in his sight. In love he predestined us to be adopted as his sons through Jesus Christ, in accordance with his pleasure and will—to the praise of his glorious grace, which he has freely given us in the One he loves.

EPHESIANS 1:3–6

Before I was born the LORD called me;
  from my birth he has made mention of my name.

ISAIAH 49:1

The Spirit himself testifies with our spirit that we are God's children. Now if we are children, then we are heirs—heirs of God and co-heirs with Christ.

ROMANS 8:16–17

Both the one who makes men holy and those who are made holy are of the same family. So Jesus is not ashamed to call them brothers.

HEBREWS 2:11

To all who received him, to those who believed in his name, he gave the right to become children of God— children born not of natural descent, nor of human decision or a husband's will, but born of God.

JOHN 1:12–13

It is within [our] inner stillness that our Father can speak to us most clearly. It is there alone with him that he becomes real to our inner intuition of spirit. It is there we begin to "see" him most acutely with the perception of our awakened conscience in response to his Word. There we sense and know his Presence. He interacts with us in our deepening conviction through his wondrous Word and by his gracious Spirit.

For the man or woman who comes to know and love God as Father in such intimacy, the times of solitude are the most exquisite in all of life. They are *"a rendezvous with the Beloved."* They are anticipated eagerly; awaited with acute expectancy; relished with enthusiasm. In a word, these times are highlights of life.

W. PHILLIP KELLER

GOD IS *with* US ...

EACH STEP OF OUR JOURNEY

"I love you and will never leave you never, ever, during your trials and testings."

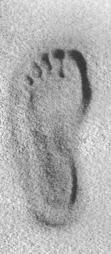

We OFTEN MAKE PROMISES we can't keep. God isn't like that. God is faithful and trustworthy. When God promises never to leave us, he means just what he says. He's not going anywhere!

"Though the mountains be shaken
*   and the hills be removed,*
yet my unfailing love for you will not be shaken
*   nor my covenant of peace be removed,"*
*   says the LORD, who has compassion on you.*

ISAIAH 54:10

Praise be to the LORD, to God our Savior,
*   who daily bears our burdens.*

PSALM 68:19

He will not let your foot slip—
*   he who watches over you will not slumber. …*
The LORD watches over you—
*   the LORD is your shade at your right hand;*
the sun will not harm you by day,
*   nor the moon by night.*
The LORD will keep you from all harm—
*   he will watch over your life;*
the LORD will watch over your coming and going
*   both now and forevermore.*

PSALM 121:3, 5−8

Do not forget this one thing, dear friends: With the Lord a day is like a thousand years, and a thousand years are like a day. The Lord is not slow in keeping his promise, as some understand slowness.

2 PETER 3:8–9

May God himself, the God of peace, sanctify you through and through. May your whole spirit, soul and body be kept blameless at the coming of our Lord Jesus Christ. The one who calls you is faithful and he will do it.

1 THESSALONIANS 5:23–24

I am still confident of this:
I will see the goodness of the LORD
in the land of the living.
Wait for the LORD;
be strong and take heart
and wait for the LORD.

PSALM 27:13–14

I was young and now I am old,
yet I have never seen the righteous forsaken
or their children begging bread.
They are always generous and lend freely;
their children will be blessed.

PSALM 37:25–26

When it seems that life is whirling out of control, we can take comfort in God's sovereignty and power. He has everything under control. And he will work his will in every circumstance.

Many are the plans in a man's heart,
but it is the LORD's purpose that prevails.

PROVERBS 19:21

I know that you can do all things, God;
no plan of yours can be thwarted.

JOB 42:2

"I am God, and there is no other;
I am God, and there is none like me.
I make known the end from the beginning,
from ancient times, what is still to come.
I say: My purpose will stand,
and I will do all that I please."

ISAIAH 46:9–10

I know that everything God does will endure forever;
nothing can be added to it and nothing taken from it.
God does it so that men will revere him.

ECCLESIASTES 3:14

The earth is the LORD's, and everything in it,
    the world, and all who live in it.

PSALM 24:1

The living may know that the Most High is sovereign
over the kingdoms of men and gives them to anyone he
wishes and sets over them the lowliest of men.

DANIEL 4:17

The LORD Almighty has purposed, and who can
    thwart him?
    His hand is stretched out, and who can turn it back?

ISAIAH 14:27

I will come and proclaim your mighty acts,
    O Sovereign LORD;
    I will proclaim your righteousness, yours alone.
Since my youth, O God, you have taught me,
    and to this day I declare your marvelous deeds.
Even when I am old and gray,
    do not forsake me, O God,
till I declare your power to the next generation,
    your might to all who are to come.

PSALM 71:16–18

Whenever we hit rock-bottom, we can be assured of God's love and care. His encouragement breathes new possibilities into impossible circumstances.

Commit your way to the LORD;
  trust in him and he will do this:
He will make your righteousness shine like the dawn,
  the justice of your cause like the noonday sun.

PSALM 37:5–6

In you, O LORD, I have taken refuge;
  let me never be put to shame;
  deliver me in your righteousness.

PSALM 31:1

My flesh and my heart may fail,
  but God is the strength of my heart
  and my portion forever.

PSALM 73:26

The LORD is with me; I will not be afraid.

PSALM 118:6

If God is for us, who can be against us?

ROMANS 8:31

The LORD will go before you,
  the God of Israel will be your rear guard.

ISAIAH 52:12

"Listen to me, …
you whom I have upheld since you were conceived,
*   and have carried since your birth.*
Even to your old age and gray hairs
*   I am he, I am he who will sustain you.*
I have made you and I will carry you;
*   I will sustain you and I will rescue you,"*
*   says the LORD.*

ISAIAH 46:3–4

In Luke 2:22–35 we meet Simeon, a man who has grown old waiting for the Messiah—the consolation of Israel. As he takes the infant Jesus into his arms, Simeon sings his praise to God. …

It was good news to finally be able to embrace the Promised One. But far and away the best news of all is that he embraces us. That was the reason for his coming. Most of us describe our coming to faith by saying, "I've asked Jesus into my life." We should really say he has invited us into his life!

That was the reason for Simeon's song. Deep inside his tired old heart, he knew that the infant he held in his arms was in truth the One who had been holding him all his life long.

MICHAEL CARD

GOD IS *with* US ...

AS OUR POWERFUL SAVIOR

"When you saw only one set of footprints
it was then that I carried you."

I AM DEEPLY MOVED WHEN I hear accounts of what the poem "Footprints" has meant to someone. Following the 1990–91 Persian Gulf crisis, for instance, I read a newspaper account of a young self-effacing Marine from Tennessee who risked his life in an Iraqi minefield. He miraculously survived. The next morning, the tankers and their crew studied the terrain, and found seven mines and some tripwires alongside his footprints. They told him he was either the stupidest or the luckiest Marine alive.

Lance-Corporal Mark Schrader told his buddies, and later the media, "I didn't see any tripwires!" Afterwards, squad members talked about the incident and someone mentioned the poem "Footprints." "It was obviously not my footprints that went through that minefield," the young hero maintains. "It was God. He carried me."

That story alone has made it all worthwhile. …

What God has done for me, what He did for the young Marine, God will do for anyone who asks Him to walk with them through life.

"I am the LORD, the God of all mankind. Is anything too hard for me?"

"See now that I myself am He!
  There is no god besides me.
I put to death and I bring to life,
    I have wounded and I will heal,
    and no one can deliver out of my hand,
      says the Lord."

DEUTERONOMY 32:39

God does as he pleases
    with the powers of heaven
    and the peoples of the earth.
No one can hold back his hand
    or say to him: "What have you done?"

DANIEL 4:35

Wealth and honor come from you;
    you are the ruler of all things.
In your hands are strength and power
    to exalt and give strength to all.
Now, our God, we give you thanks,
    and praise your glorious name.

1 CHRONICLES 29:12–13

My soul finds rest in God alone;
    my salvation comes from him.
He alone is my rock and my salvation;
    he is my fortress, I will never be shaken.

PSALM 62:1–2

Our problems may seem overwhelming, but God's power is stronger than any obstacle we may face.

"Be still, and know that I am God;
*   I will be exalted among the nations,*
*   I will be exalted in the earth."*
The LORD Almighty is with us;
*   the God of Jacob is our fortress.*

PSALM 46:10–11

The LORD is slow to anger and great in power. …
His way is in the whirlwind and the storm,
*   and clouds are the dust of his feet.*

NAHUM 1:3

I can do everything through Christ who gives me strength.

PHILIPPIANS 4:13

Be strong in the Lord and in his mighty power.

EPHESIANS 6:10

The eternal God is your refuge,
*   and underneath are the everlasting arms.*

DEUTERONOMY 33:27

We can be assured that [God] is in control of every aspect of our lives. He will prepare the way before us. He will never leave us. And he will provide our every need.

My God will meet all your needs according to his glorious riches in Christ Jesus.

PHILIPPIANS 4:19

"Before they call I will answer;
    while they are still speaking I will hear,"
        says the LORD.

ISAIAH 65:24

Jesus said, "If you believe, you will receive whatever you ask for in prayer."

MATTHEW 21:22

No eye has seen, no ear has heard, no mind has conceived what God has prepared for those who love him.

1 CORINTHIANS 2:9

Taste and see that the LORD is good;
    blessed is the man who takes refuge in him.

PSALM 34:8

O LORD Almighty,
    blessed is the man who trusts in you.

PSALM 84:12

Blessed is he whose help is the God of Jacob,
    whose hope is in the LORD his God,
the Maker of heaven and earth,
    the sea, and everything in them—
    the LORD, who remains faithful forever.

PSALM 146:5−6

God who did not spare his own Son, but gave him up
for us all—how will he not also, along with him, gra-
ciously give us all things?

ROMANS 8:32

Praise the LORD, O my soul,
    and forget not all his benefits—
who forgives all your sins
    and heals all your diseases,
who redeems your life from the pit
    and crowns you with love and compassion,
who satisfies your desires with good things
    so that your youth is renewed like the eagle's.

PSALM 103:2−5

Jesus said, "Whoever drinks the water I give him will
never thirst. Indeed, the water I give him will become
in him a spring of water welling up to eternal life."

JOHN 4:14

As [God] carries us over the rough places in our lives, he speaks words of peace and blessing.

The LORD bless you
and keep you;
the LORD make his face shine upon you
and be gracious to you;
the LORD turn his face toward you
and give you peace.

NUMBERS 6:24–26

May the God of peace … equip you with everything good for doing his will, and may he work in us what is pleasing to him, through Jesus Christ, to whom be glory for ever and ever. Amen.

HEBREWS 13:20–21

God molds us and makes us and holds us in his hand. No matter what happens in this life, I'm in his hand. What a mighty God we serve! Right or wrong, up or down, poverty or wealth, sickness or health, come what may, I am in his hand. Hallelujah, I am in his hand.

H. BEECHER HICKS

ACKNOWLEDGEMENTS

Exerpts Taken From:

The Men's Devotional Bible: New International Version.
©1993 by The Zondervan Corporation. All rights reserved.

Bridges, Jerry. *The Practice of Godliness.* © 1983 by Jerry Bridges.
Used by permission of NavPress.

Card, Michael. *Immanuel: Reflections On The Life Of Christ.* ©1990
Michael Card. Used by permission of Thomas Nelson Publishing.

Halverson, Richard. *Perspective.* © 1957, 1985 by Cowman Publishing Company. Used by permission of The Zondervan Corporation.

Hicks, Beecher, H. *Correspondence With A Cripple From Tarsus.* ©
1990 by H. Beecher Hicks. Used by permission of The Zondervan
Corporation.

Hybels, Bill. *Honest to God?* © 1990 by Bill Hybels. Used by permission of The Zondervan Corporation.

Hybels, Bill. *Who You Are When No One Is Looking.* ©1987 by Bill
Hybels. Used by permission of InterVarsity Press. Downers Grove, Il.

Keller, W. Phillip. *God Is My Delight.* © 1991 by W. Phillip Keller
and published by Kregel Publications. Grand Rapids, MI. Used by
permission.

Lockerbie, D. Bruce. *Fatherlove.* © 1981 by D. Bruce Lockerbie. Used
by permission of Doubleday, a division of Bantam Doubleday Dell
Publishing Group

Tozer, A. W. *Renewed Day By Day.* © 1980 by Christian Publications. Used by permission.

Welch, Reuben R. *Let's Listen To Jesus.* © 1985, 1988 by The Zondervan Corporation. *Faith For The Journey.* © 1988 by Reuben R.
Welch. Used by permission of The Zondervan Corporation

Yancey, Philip. *Disappointment With God.* Copyright © 1988 by
Philip Yancey. Used by permission of The Zondervan Corporation.

At Inspirio we love to hear from you—
your stories, your feedback,
and your product ideas.
Please send your comments to us
by way of e-mail at
icares@zondervan.com
or to the address below:

inspirio

Attn: Inspirio Cares
5300 Patterson Avenue SE
Grand Rapids, MI 49530

If you would like further information
about Inspirio and the products we
create please visit us at:
www.inspiriogifts.com

Thank you and God Bless!